AFTER A LOST ORIGINAL

OTHER BOOKS BY DAVID SHAPIRO

Poetry

January
Poems from Deal
A Man Holding an Acoustic Panel
The Page-turner
Lateness
To An Idea
House (Blown Apart)

Criticism

An Introduction to John Ashbery's Poetry
Jim Dine: Painting What One Is
Jasper Johns' Drawings
Mondrian: Flowers

Also

An Anthology of New York Poets
    (with R. Padgett)
The Selected Poems of Jacques Dupin
    (with P. Auster)
The Writings of Robert and Sonia Delaunay
    (with Arthur A. Cohen)
Alfred Leslie: The Killing Cycle
    (with J. Stein)
The Eight Names of Picasso by Rafael
    Alberti (with G. Berns)
The Collapse of Time (with J. Hejduk)

AFTER A LOST ORIGINAL

A Book of Poems

DAVID SHAPIRO

THE OVERLOOK PRESS
WOODSTOCK • NEW YORK

Some of these poems have appeared in American Poetry Review, Boulevard, Broadway II, Architectures, New Observations, The Forward, Scripsi, New American Writing, Shiny, Oblek, The Literary Review, St. Mark's Newsletter, Notus, Pataphysics, A + U, and Conjunctions

"After a Lost Original" appeared with an etching by Terry Winters in a special edition by Solo Press.

"The Seasons" appeared in The Best American Poetry, 1991.

Some of these poems have appeared in Japanese and English in a volume on St. Clair Cemin, Art Random, Kyoto, Japan.

"The Uncertainty" appeared in a volume, *1979-1989 American, Italian, Mexican Art,* Hofstra University, Hofstra Museum.

The poem, "For Victims," in a slightly different form, appeared in *Blood To Remember*, edited by Charles Fishman.

The author thanks the Graham Foundation for help on this and other projects.

Some of the poems were used as text for Rudy Burckhardt's film, "Great Natural Flavor," shown at the Lincoln Center Film Festival, 1991. "God Meets the Angel," "The Boss Poem," and "A Desert Rose" were written in collaboration with Daniel Shapiro.

First published in 1994 by
The Overlook Press
Lewis Hollow Road
Woodstock, New York 12498

Copyright © David Shapiro

All Rights Reserved. No part of this publication may be reproduced or transmitted in any form or by any means, electronic or mechanical, including photocopy, recording, or any information storage and retrieval system now known or to be invented without permission in writing from the publisher, except by a reviewer who wishes to quote brief passages in connection with a review written for inclusion in a magazine, newspaper, or broadcast.

Library of Congress Cataloging-in-Publication Data

Shapiro, David, 1947–
After a lost original : a book of poems / David Shapiro.
p. cm.
1. Title.
PS3569.H34A69 1994
811'.54—dc20
93-44117
CIP

Book Design by Bernard Schleifer
Typeset in Garamond by AeroType, Inc.
ISBN: 0-87951-527-9
35798642
First Edition

Contents

AFTER A LOST ORIGINAL

After a Lost Original 11
The Snow Is Alive 12
Walter Benjamin: A Lost Poem 13
In Germany 14
After *Asturiana* 15
You Are Tall and Thin 16
Prayer for my Son 17
To My Son 20
House of the Secret 21
For Victims 22

BROKEN OBJECTS, DISCARDED LANDSCAPE

After 25
A Part for the Part 26
Broken Objects, Discarded Landscape 27
Dido to Aeneas 28
Goofy Plays Second Fiddle in the Family Quartet 30
Sentences 31
Lucidity 32
You Are The You 33
A Dream 34
Untitled Dreams 35
"The Dead Will Not Praise You" 36
A Problem and Its Solution 37
A Note about the Author 38

HOUSE 39

VOICE

Voice 55
A Night of Criticism 56
The Mistranslation 57

A Polaroid as Big as a Tapestry 58
Dreams of a Young Architect 59
Friday's Word 60
God Meets the Angel 61
The Boss Poem 62
A Lost Poem 63
Psalm 64
For Borges: Spinoza 65
An Evening Without Criticism 66
Problems of the Moon 67
The Uncertainty 68
A Private Embrace 69
A Note and Poem by Joe Ceravolo in a Dream 70
A Desert Rose 72

MULTIPLE SUNS 73

THE SEASONS 79

for my son Daniel

AFTER A LOST ORIGINAL

After a Lost Original

When the translation and the original meet
The doubtful original and the strong mistranslation
The original feels lost like a triple pun
And the translation cries, Without me you are lost
Then be my dream, thin as the definition
Of a trance in a garden
The ambiguous friend responds, Perhaps I do astonish you
Like a boy confused with a butterfly's dream
But you are my dream now, after all
If I don't think of you, you disappear
After which they both comically disappear
Like a slice through two trees for a thousand years
Return knowing coldly a need for guerdons, guardians
Letters written on clouds, snakes on curtains and naked devices
Frighten them no longer since they live only together
Father and son refracted through blue green black moss
They travel together to the margins of a cloud

The Snow is Alive

I

The snow is alive

But my son cries

The snow is not alive
The snow cannot speak!
The snow cannot come inside!
You cannot break the snow!

But the snow is alive

And the tree is angry

II

I was afraid into again.
Where can I find you,
Tall flower, redolent
Of the divided spring?

Walter Benjamin: A Lost Poem

after a dream

In a lost essay on poetry, Walter Benjamin had written, *I was born into a rich, perhaps too-rich and too comfortable existence in Berlin. Each time my family saw soot in the air we wanted to move to another vacation spot. Poetry today withholds too much. What does it withhold. At any rate, eclecticism, Prokofiev . . .* The most Brechtian poem of Benjamin has almost been forgotten. It was published under the title *David*, with a section of a door knob as a slightly Duchampian typographic oddity. I found the proofs, rare as the Redon for *A Throw of the Dice*, in a bookstore. The poem was fairly simple:

> David or King David
> How
> did you
> *done*
> your door

Unfortunately, many of Benjamin's remarks on poetry were now simple scratches on the cover of the book, effaced like the infamous magic writing pad and indecipherable as hidden love (as opposed to open rebuke). Some of his lost short stories appear in this volume. Scholem said, There was nothing like being alone with Walter Benjamin. *It made one want to read.* The source of that remark is also lost.

In Germany

I did not mount Mt. Parnassus
Nor could I walk Philosopher's Walk
    It was too high (altus—also reversed)
        Or too late (or—not yet)
I took your way
But halfway there (oh Germany it *was* insane)
   Wanted my own: Narcissus Narcissus
   Then the blue glides off the page

          The beam with its probing lip moved across us
            Recording our model travels

Language in your mouth—fiery as a tongue
Like a flower deleted by a whirling pencil

   We are the sculptors now, making our own doors
   The words remain, but the gods are gone for good

The idea remains, but the words are gone like gods

After Asturiana

On the road to a door
On the way to a window

I saw nothing like a soul
Only the dust in competition

Lifted by the air
That was like a sailor joking

Nothing carried to nothing
A sailor was bouncing

In the world's salt: Now dance!
Now you are dancing like the world

Nothing equals nothing like a word
I get lost and make mistakes in your grace

You are Tall and Thin

In the circle of the sky
I disembark quietly: You were wrong.

They call this the street
Where a single dove made a difference, where we galloped
over each other like car tires.

The song says, You are tall and thin
like your mother.
In the sentence that follows, you sell
my dirty body.

Does it hurt to mix yourself up with conquistadors
So many hands, so many javelins, so many burials
like the photograph of an error.

Throughout the night, the song thinks
this is it
And often you live like a simulation
shopping for eyes.

I crossed the riddle,
Caring about the colors, water purple and orange.

Plunging like an elevator into an envelope
All these letters, your branches, fragrant Rhada.

While I wake slowly as a child
You are tall and thin on the bed where
you play so well.

You are high and delegate authority
like a lake.
The night dies like a ninny on the wall.

At night you burn like the library of Alexandria.
In the morning you are Alexandria, in a mirror.

You are so black you are white, like a firefly in sunlight.

Prayer for my Son

There is no storm
But the gods are hid
Like a baby
Under an archaic coverlid
The hated father
Like a punitive hill
I am the obstacle
The music of the radioactive wind
Inappropriately hoping
To have prayed
Appropriating the grammar
Of another mind
Have a year in a prayer
A year in an hour
Stars glisten
Outside the window of the tower
The bridge has no scream
Detail it
The architecture of chaos
In the stream
Be a string musician
Battering on a drum
Is like riding
The chances of the sea
The Dalai Lama says Be kind
No maybe
The Russian says Humiliate no one

A friend is better
Than friendship
The Fool speaks the truth
A gun is a false spray
Rats emerge from the sun
In an odd way
Be fastidious as you want but eat
And avoid the contaminated meat

Of governments serving us up
As if we were underdone
Forget what you have earned
Learn to know
What you have not yet learned
Until you confuse the good
With the beautiful
Don't seek out the wise, be wise
Never abandon the beloved
Just close your eyes
To the world and open your eyes

Be concealed
Like a conceptual tree
And when you need to be explicit, be
But watch out for the right cliché
At the wrong moment like the aleatory sound
That hunts you down for an easy chase
Avoid an easy quarrel like a laurel
Stay at the typewriter only to remember
That heaven is a clear place

The Angel of Silesia ought to know
It is not parody you will have loved
Or the hysterical search
To be approved
Other proverbs: Let her be late
And you be on time to beat me up
But without hate
Try to become the prudent imprudent chief
For the oxymoronic sting of a mind
That completely pursues
And presses the redness
Into a leaf
A too cerebral frustrated love's
The worst
By which all late Romantics

Are accursed
So try to see the third coming
My first born
And drink out of the sexual horn
With a low opinion of mad monist mind
That calls false coherence a good
And forgets every color
In the manifold wind
Though anxiety cannot be driven hence
Learn the pleasure
Of poetic radiance
Each artist in each other artist delighting
Opposed to the combat
Of the self-affrighting

Do not be a suicide
Of some professor's self-anointed will
Forget the paternal maternal scowl
Forget the bric-a-brac
Of an infantile howl
Be happy in godless arms
Be happier still
I wanted you, we wanted you only
To be happier in your house
Than those crucified
By the falsely ceremonious
Let pride come upon you unawares
Like a traveller
Who always has the fares
In a pocket without precedent
And even without money
It will be as if you were
That second born
Each note will issue
Clearly from the nonsymbolic horn
You will rest upon her
As if you were a tree.

To my Son

> *King Oedipus has one eye too many, perhaps.*
> HÖLDERLIN

I love you so much
I am going to let you kill me.
Pathos your thin arms your
neck your hair rich
without perfume
and your eyes bright as a brooch
You say you will kill me tomorrow
and I believe you
but for now you must sleep
in my arms like a cheat at cards
Five years we have lived together
counting like the Chinese
I fear every narrow road
on which we will eventually meet
But do not banish me so fast, my son
Your clubfoot that I have pierced
is more beautiful, to me, than your mother's breast.

House of the Secret

I met the old dead poet
And told him I no longer loved my work
As I had when a child or even fifteen
Sorry I had not written someone else's poem but it was already written

He told me, Never think of others or of yourself
Never do anything for others or for yourself
And never write poetry for another or for yourself
Or yourselves

The secret hangs from the top, like a prayer on a branch
It is the house of secrets, narrowing to the last story
Or the house of the secret, singular
And I wept, wondering where he had concealed such bitter sense

The camera was hidden under the floor like a boat
The poem hung from the branch above the silver bridge
Criticism that does not end, even in Paradise
We think it is a bridge because it is silver. It is not a bridge.
Lost is lost.

For Victims

They have used the bodies of children
As improvised bridges,
Which they later cross.
First the sun and the moon,
Then the earth comes in.
But they have lost
The atmosphere, which belongs to them

Light passersby

BROKEN OBJECTS, DISCARDED LANDSCAPE

1. *After*

There is the gate or the copy of a gate
Blood outlines the gate, like a nude
A pink flower like a tree emits sparks
They gather into a yellow blue fragmentary flower
In the other space, formed by flowers torn apart
It bites the ground, like a blackened moon
Blood outlines a few jagged petals
Where does this flower emerge if not from history
The night-flower beside it is not dark enough with
Turmoil of strokes, with labor of **having been there**
The night-flower explodes, is blue less
Relentless, should there be nothing but shadow
The twentieth century falls off below and fragility
And the kitsch of flowers above, finesse of heaven
No one can enter here, and there is nothing but hope

2. *A Part for the Part*

I demur. What was Gomorrah's crime?
Parodying, parodying, parodying?
That grotesque moment when I realize I am flying like a firefly
beneath the frozen, inverted earth
in the shadow of the shadow of a cassette
Oh door to the door

3. Broken Objects,
Discarded Landscape

A novelist took a vacation with me.
She ate breakfast in my old house like a sister.
She asked me to play chamber music but only for a moment
Then found another way to waste the afternoon alone.

We ignored the immense museum—
Those frightened by space those by nearness walked quickly
    together.
I asked her what she thought of all this work on paper.
Form inhuman form she cried though I begged her to hear a voice
    I was apologizing for my whole life

But the world could not come to a reading.
She pointed to a logical fallacy there the world thick with
Broken objects, discarded landscape.
But I said your face her face was thin with light and weightless.

She was the narrator all right.
But she was also the sacrifice.
Thus if I painted double helixes she would call it
Abstract but I would be painting life itself.

4. *Dido to Aeneas*

(after Hart and Osborn)

I.

It was words that detained us, though they do not reach
I was devoted to the future and you like a yellow acanthus
You wanted to bend to some more obvious bed
Sychaeus was abolished after a desuetude
The night also betrayed me but I drew it out
and I asked you many things about very strong Hector
You were my guest and I loved narrative
like an error on the land of all fluctuating seas
And you apostrophized as if from a need
Night rushed down with the stars like analogies
Now when I look up there is only a chaos like a cave
You have become Rome, while I became something like music
You exchanged me for a fate or a work
drinking like long love but I will tell you now nothing

II.

Everyone has been silent but you are attentive
May you have an immense exile like a surface
A god pulled you to my coast in a digression
Everyone wishes to say things even the air
But you have thrown your arms around the image's neck
And escaped alone with your hands: you and I would become the same cave
The mountains do they present anything
Nor am I copying you now king of the obsessed doors
I believed you and the equivocations
If only the earth had opened or I could go toward images
I began to speak but I stop in the middle
Alone in the vapid room I could hear you and touch the bed like a relic
My towers did not rise, discontinuity equalled the sky,
Day was a cause a name is a screen and we have called it secret love

III.

It was the night of tired-out bodies
With a placid sleep giving access to other bodies
The woods are like a sieve and the sky is normal
The stars revolve like lovers in their lapses
Each leaf on the field is quiet like a variegated birth
And the birds in many colors occupy the lakes
Which occupy the fields and the little rough brambles
But the unhappy mind is like a double Thebes on stage
May our shores combine against your shores
It is possible to hate life and throw it off like a nurse
Oh dear nurse please send me my sister
I have lived and I have finished now I am a big image
I am a city and a statue and a wall and a revenge
It is a recent cut like an accident in a forest

IV.

You always wanted the most favorable time to speak
and I have found the time not to speak
You think you will have names but I follow in sequence
You wanted to see but you cannot even see the cave
But you had to come to Hell and the urns of secret writing
You think you see something and you see the extreme sequitur
This was the last time you said you would address me
By permission and how much you loved permission the word
My eyes can do something else nor do I exist the joke
You are not even interesting as a cliff or a flight into waves
I will hurry away to the one who equals my love
And you will win Aeneas Rome but not Dido
It is not the irresponsible silence of a suicide
But I had the right to the cry without translation

5. *Goofy Plays Second Fiddle in the Family Quartet*

> Evil is a proof of God, says Goofy
> And I know I'm just a cartoon character
> I know I can't write monologues
> Like my friend Mickey, But I'm tired
> Of being ink, I'm tired of being music
> Splashed against trees
> And when I go I'll go like leaves into houses
> I'll go like color, I'll go
> Like my friend Mickey. In a dream
> I saw a Dead Street Sign.
> My feet seemed tied around my waist.
> I was a prisoner of Outer Forces again.

The big crossword puzzle lit up inside;
What is Goofy's first name? But you all know
It was Dippy Dog and then The Goof.
Minnie was a toxicology student,
Because Mickey was toxic. He was so toxic
He stayed in bed all day, like a painter.

> And my friend sang monologues on the phone
> So sweetly, I thought
> I was on an island. But never wake
> He cried and certainly never wake
> Inside a dream and certainly never wake
> Inside a poem.
> You all know my original name,
> But do you know my name now?

6. Sentences

It is raining in my heart, but I don't believe that it is raining.
It is raining softly on the town, but I don't believe the town exists.
It is raining softly on the tip of my tongue, but not now.
You say it is a sentence, but there is some possibility it is not a sentence.
It is a sentence, but it is very difficult to explain why it is a sentence.

My love is on the phone, but it is not now that my love is on the phone.
I have moved, but I do not know that I have moved.
I am in a position to assert the summer has ended, but I don't believe it.
A raven screamed at one in the parking lot, but it was not a raven; it was a prisoner.
My love is a double agent, and I hesitantly believe she is not.

Time is brutal, but I do not believe time is brutal.
Fact: Time is a brutal fact, but it is not certain time is a brutal fact.
Fact: Time is a social animal, but it may be that time is not a social animal.
Time satisfies all these conditions, but time does not satisfy all.
Time depends on future sentences: What I find hard to believe.

The book contains your barest preface, but I do not think it is a book.
The table of contents is unhelpful, but I do not think it is the contents.
Worst of all there is a key, but I believe there is no key.
The reader loses his way richly, but it is not certain that the reader loses.
Nevertheless, you found your way about, though I do not know you.

7. *Lucidity*

Sleep with the moon and receive a poem
Maybe we were all born
a little too "up"
There is such a thing as temperament a visit
shocked quartz opaque dreaming
shocked because the earth received catastrophe
like a joyful eye
that clarifies and tolerates each lamp

8. *You Are The You*

You are the you in this poem,
Mon amour.
Harrisburg mon amour.
Boats break.

So-and-so asked me,
To whom does the you in your poem
Refer.
I said, Are you feeling well, So-and-so.

I can't believe I said.
It. So sue me.
I said, It's the beloved, So-and-so.
Oh is that all.

Well, I said, she wouldn't think
It was so little.
To look up into your face
Is like looking into the devastated stars.

Lights of all kinds I traced,
You and you and you and you.
You are the you of this poem, mon amour.
Boats break.

9. *A Dream*

Fairfield Porter, 1907–1975

You, me
with moistened lips
we kissed
by the stopwatch
as in the movies
"film time fifteen
minutes"
then my sister on the porch
said Fairfield are you cerebrating
Fairfield came out of the window
("stuck his head out")
and then we began to
question him
He said that the world
after death was wonderful
as the world was wonderful
and that there were no
explanations in this one
just as in a good poem
When I looked for
a piece of paper
it was already titled
"A Family Reunion."

10. *Untitled Dreams*

The painter is deposing my poetry. He says that he works
from 9 to 5 every day, not mere painting, but thinking "outside."
He says that my poetry is too "either/or" whereas the best art
is "just and." He also thinks that I have purposely made my poetry
coherent to get the other members of the so-called School drunk
(or to make them look drunk? I cannot remember). I realize with
a shudder how much he dislikes my poetry. I say, But, painter,
that is just what was said about you, in a sense, in relation to
an expressionism, that you took it and made it something curiously
coherent like the United States of America. No response.

My "Hospital City"
I walk down the corridor to my hospital's room.
She is lying unconsciously slouched in a chair. A nurse
is cutting her hair, what little there is, from her almost
completely bald skull. My mother.

11. "The Dead Will Not Praise You"

Cantor Berele Chagy

My grandfather emerges
in a synagogue
with familiar accents
unlike his noble voice
a pudgy little man
sweet tenor coloratura flautando
He marches down the aisle
with a blue white crown
Women ask questions
and they are charmed
and he is beloved
like etymology
Is my mother in attendance
or is she dead?
What are questions now?
Are the dead permitted: to
sing? Is he serious?
Are the dead permitted
to return and sing?

12. A Problem and Its Solution

Part of a woman holds a boy
With her left arm
There is preserved only a part of her chest
The child is frightened and clings to her breast

What is carved is careful and dry
The century is ending, uncertainty falls on her shoulders
Like the original rich hair
They have armed Aphrodite

Long and glossy and dark green
And semisucculent, the narcissus has broken
Love, love, part child part dirt
Most fragrant long after signs of human habitation

To stain the violin
Such minor differences are lustre
Sea of fecundity, sea of nectar, sea of crimes
Scratched by a thumbnail, scratched by a soft pin

13. *A Note about the Author*

Or "Not Writing A Novel"
A range of grey mountains
cannot obscure my love
for you and Poetry
though I have failed in both
Is it true that
my last lines are always too much like
last lines?

Oh sun hiding
Then not hiding
like a bright round
word next to a
player of games
even behind a player

Now you are working again but on edge
behind green maples, elms, local names
But let's not be too delicate
A bird on the roof of a warehouse

Could I learn to play a four-dimensional
game like this one

The train starts down the river like a regionalist
Banks like tombs, tombs like banks
Pigeons like dancers, dancers like pigeons
The sun has this effect through dirty windows

But language is not a pencil
Is it true
that language is not our pencil
True and false
Language is not a pencil

How far away you are in paradise, like smoke

HOUSE

1.

In extreme pain
Q meets T
They walk into a house
And later, a double exposure is sent to S

Somewhere behind the curtains
Uncertainty is laughing
As you ask the yes or no questions
I am moving towards you by analogy

2. A Prayer

You have grown up the liveliest ghost
After all, you are not following chamber music
    Friday nights
in or reading newsy novels from the library
You have become a voice, more read now than reading

As one avoids your name but starts out
    singing it in travel
Our father, emphasis on our elder betters
with the pronouns not possessed but stolen like
    a royal teacup
Thy will be done, since we have little faith that
    ours ever could

On earth and heaven: two truncated rhomboids
Give up this day, give us one day, give it
Like water, and also give us water
Snow, music and house I now avoid, as one avoids
    certain words, and they are words.

3.

This then is a possible house
This then is a possible Novel
How I have detested you, sleep
The giddy bellboy at the top of the
    hotel
Shuddering like an elevator
Yes it is all about itself, yourself
Anticipatory elegy
Anticipating the elegies
The window like a smoking igloo
    window
Opening on an expanded vocabulary
    of ice
The leaves my sister played in
The interior is a complete lie
and incomplete
Every day another novel
Since one cannot rise into sleep

4.

What about an open mouth
Prince Myshkin was trying to cross the street
without hurting anybody
It's hard to make out Myshkin on the phonograph
Music for the idiots
Hedda Gabler tried to shoot me also
No, no, don't!
And don't keep me writing the dissertations
    on stage directions
In obeisance to the bloated judge
Who will more or less tawdrily judge us
On some respective Judgment Day
Somewhat more softly sweep the string
A jocular if Goethean task
The window is profoundly closed as a death mask
The eyes closed always on the word
Pink is distributed through the universe
And then the owner relents
The universe is "let go"
Clouds are shunted quickly through surgery
Stars, vacuous events, elevators in the air, last notes
One strand of hair was music
And later it doesn't fall like a finger
What's all of this talk about snow for
Apollo sits on the house with Cassandra thinking
We couldn't all be Scotch-taped together
Though we tried, language knows we tried
The piano knows we tried
The linden tree knows as much
And any other so-called natural instruments
Paolo's Francesca smiled her famous smile
Which I kissed all smiling, waiting
Dictating, entranced

5.

False paint on white paintbrush
Even to talk about it isn't too cloudy
Fervent window
You build and ruin everything like repetition
Even the elegiac house which you touch
    which you can't touch
which you enter which you cannot enter
Live–in help
Live–in house
Unlivable house
Unlivable snow
L'hiver dur
During most of it
Enduring most of it
With phonemes in the midst of it all
Just permutations of the phoneme
Sunspots bleeding
Beneath an oak
The page emerging from the psyche
the snow none too secretly thawing from
    the outside now

No floor
No young fate
The history of time-lapse photography
is growing now
You cannot even take dictation
You don't want this to go on
You have destroyed a little of everything
How dare you interrupt me in my house
Make music too soft to listen to
Want the bed too low
Don't even want this to exist
Want me to become unconscious
A house to sink.

6.

The white telephone
In the third-person profile
The white wicker chair
and the blue pants
The white shadowy plaster replica
    of my father and that my father
    made of you
Accurate as calipers and thus false
The desk and empty cities
The slope of maturity, the garlands of
    geniality
The hook of contempt, the stroke through
    the ego
It has all replaced palmistry
Leonardo observing the dead hand
    and the long lines of life
The white school paper and, stapled
    in the center,
The white school paper
Even the dusty persian blinds are white
but the plant is a little monstrously green
In the white corner
In the loud night

7.

In the beginning was the house
A nice sofa, inveterate tuba, and the impossible
    flow of music
It was impossible to stop the gods, more possible
    to stop the snow
The streetlight was a streetlight
To an idea was a good idea
The octaves were a drawing
Ave Maria was a drawing
The night sky was a drawing
The sky was a work on paper
Why couldn't it have been a star stapled to a
    planetarium
Not two strings together
Not Pythagoras
The beach was not going to stop, nor mussels
    black and attached to the jetty
It was awkward closing the ripped snail

You might be laughing with your whole life
Less possible to laugh here
Television was the little house
full of games and give-aways and human
    sacrifice
It was too coherent, too many tears, too
    much winglessness
Songlessness
One would look beyond it and the enclosing window
Improvising in front of the window
It would be quite different than knowing
and sustaining and dealing with it dissonantly
As if a trill could be a closure
One might as well expect what one knows
like a chin rest in a violin case

And not a piano in a park
One might as well be green and velvet
As if the broad sun were a sign
Don't go to Russia telling these secrets
about the "snow secretly thawing from within"
Dancing on your knees
Years have passed between songs
All slightly mean and suited up more than professional
Very strong, all of this to express the champagne
Secretly snow was falling within
On the top range among the toy cars
Into the summer of the superficial pool
The mistranslation of page 9
Emerging on the surface like a black pool
How much the house wanted the missing word.

8.

I am not now nor have I ever been asleep
Turning towards the portable harpsichord
Underneath the garden where a snake was sensibly shot
All of the curses were equally impressive
All of the caresses
You nodded to me on the top of a wave
And beseeched me from the undertow
Broken chords up and down the beach
Yet one more repetitious narrative
And you swam out like a honeysuckle, like
    a revised toy airplane
The child inhabits
Vacillating near the sun's waxy odors
There is no advance in the arpeggio
Very quietly now the eyes go out of business
Dido refuses to write
Everyone is growing stronger from the load of
    empty pictures

9.

Jove was a clause
Jupiter an implication
It used to be fecund gold
Gold through which the air was thrown
Wings that certainly preferred to be punctured
I was confused with your branch, with your
    olive branch
Pride, long since dry
A long time ago we dressed in leaves and suddenly
    we are ripe
Fate was the prize
Your face, a quantum, a ferocious war
Neither do I think
Neither am I born
Under the astringent gaze of the highest
    part of the whole
The house rises heavily from the ground and
    groans
In pallor the house sits like an oar
The roof is black with tar
The walls overflow with gall
The stairway is sprinkled with saffron
The door is absent
unless miseries have caused some door

10.

Stretching toward the air
as if one would be strong
Without anything to be strong upon or with
Roman à clef hardly opening oneself
Sounds from Russia rise
to the luminous surface of
How snowy a consciousness once conscience
I love the silver birch
    because it was a simple solution
I loved the sycamore
because it lacked all integrity
I loved the lake
    because it was man-made
I loved even the great globe itself on my desk
    because it predicted many deaths
A lot of changed names
The newly dead are easy to find
But the concert is hardly over though not alive

11.

In time the incredible lion took place
Ozone, oxide, sheaths of smoke by Turgenev
Wherever else it had been
Afterwards the law kept you on the pavement
Like snow situated somewhere between
Now we can put away our gondolas
What would be called beckoning from the clouds
What you are writing
    sitting on an edge.

The windows in the house are made of nylon
Through the windows one can make out a model
    of the great house of cardboard.

12.

Put the music back to the beginning.
Write that down, the impossible.
If the music turns off you'll have to
     reinstate it.
The island of Delos without the dead
All stairs—an island we must spell for you
A narrow moment narrowly cemented
Idle talk—revolted by the quadrivium
     that could be cut in glass
Dictating to blind daughters or to typewriters
Comical precursors, music to be forgotten
To play backwards on broken ice, in different tempi.

That is not it.
By now we have come upon our theme of
themelessness proper
As if meeting death half-way by a dart.
Where it most breathes I have observed
The is delicate
In search of a lost paragraph, lost lint,
the fresh word or space
But what was so famous about freshness
What was so glamorous about it as glue
Gigantic horses upon the stolen pediment
Icarus didn't fear loss of control
So much as a certain grandiosity, a certain
     what do I know.

But this could be much longer or tentative
     or substantial like syntax
Ever not quite master of those who do not know
The snow fell like spigots
Or was it from here
You might have mutilated the questions

From the point of view of every right dissolution
What the day knew or straight back to the
    cat's brain
Laughing besides home-made pillows
Home-made theodicy
But what one doesn't know are the geometries
     that might have described or created
        that possible world.

VOICE

1. Voice

A woman's voice
is a sexual organ
according to the Rabbis
I would draw your voice
photo of a sketch for
reproduction (not for sale)
A woman's voice
is a body part
again washed to the beach
like a bloody misogyny
Cold light
is misunderstood
Do the firefly
lights up from inside
a children's song
Friend meets Waldheim
Temple of Hypermnesia
are you in the
"forgetting movement"
Kitsch and poetry
No I'm in the remembrance
movement and poetry
is fire in the house

2. *A Night of Criticism*

At the end of the greatest book of poetry
all you have is a book in your hands
That is what I said to a comedian in a dream
about the word "bed" or any word for that matter
our private associations are permitted
but do not reveal themselves on the page
In a sense, one names something only not
to have it, the ruined theme of absence
A little innovation like music notated
can do a little to swell a forte
help an African scene or two
but you do not know it is this bed
poetry is not exactly affirmative
like thick description in anthropology
jargon that makes a movie of our lives
snow at the window and a child in our arms
looking at the snow for the first time
like a realist in a corridor for the winter
forced to fix the swiftly falling buildings
incongruous as a cloud

3. The Mistranslation

Negative sounds on top of the forest.
I see words in the deep moss,
conversation in the lichen.
The mountain hears bright shadows shine.
A mountain brightens; shadows shine.
I hear the mountains; bright shadows shine.
But I am empty, and return to return again.
    Blue green black moss.

                              (after Weinberger's Wang Wei)

4. *A Polaroid as Big as a Tapestry*

You who are just eyes
Everyone hates love
Because it has designs on one like Wordsworth's
    poetry
And because it is something medical like a
    wish
Now they've invented a pill but they didn't
    invent love at night
So haggard and so woebegone
You I love are not even a telephone call away
Beside me in the night in which I have become
    nothing
Which let us hope is an exaggeration of an
    attenuation
As you had my hearing tested
And the music went up to 2 platinum
    place 1500 cycles cycling
Love is making you feel bad in the museums
Like the magic sound that protects dead
    painting
Like the Venus that couldn't be by Poussin
Because she is too thin
And so much for connoisseurship
You were always studying too much
Like Narcissus in the Wildenstein Gallery
Leaning over the green pool of blue paint
Where they treat you like a thief and you are
    a thief too
Each kiss more interesting than everything

5. *Dreams of a Young Architect*

You were reading Tess of the D'Urbervilles.
And you were drying your hair at the same time.
You pulled the plug out of the wall by the cord
And the cord separated from the plug, which remained
    in the wall.

As a sapphire is dear to the planet of Saturn,
And if to get is a very general term, you have
    gotten through.
And we were getting along, meeting our needs as a
    vacuum tube does it.
Then we came to this place of mental and spiritual
    suffering.

We twined about each other like real numbers,
    with a difference in pitch.
You tasted tentatively this preening brooch
And sipped some plain tequila inside your teepee.
I played on my primitive xylophone, you resonated
    beneath each bar and an unexpected piccolo came
        floating alone.

The stars raced ahead like teams, each team member
Covering specified portions of the sky, releasing icy light.
The clouds walked past like pedestrians to the side
    of the street.
As the snake throws his body forward in the pale-colored
    desert in a series of loops.

6. *Friday's Word*

**Suddenly I saw all this crawling out of
the morning glory like things**

There is a **glory** in morning glory
and a **grimy igloo**, too,
where a moron rooms, all moony
looking for the one form of a roomy word

The morning glory lurches out of the back
of the **lorry** while the drivers
sing their **lingo** into the island **gloom**
It is a **minor irony** of the island that

the most one can do to relax this **rigor**
is to be **going**, adding s's to words
and trying out all disallowed foreigners
Answers tomorrow, sighs the distended **groom**

to the bride with his **loony groin**
pressing against her like five red letters
—for example, swing or swung, not both—
but she knows he is **lying** at least eighteen times

7. *God Meets the Angel*

—with Daniel

Flying with my flying wings
flying in my flying wings
I'm flying and I'm going to see God
I'm going to see God now

*

I say God is everywhere

*

Angels sleep
I know what angels start with
A
They sleep in a flower
Angels are so little
God is little
like milkweed
like little seeds

*

God is like little seeds
They're growing God
The wings are purple and silver
They feel heavy
as milkweed
heavy with stones

8. The Boss Poem

—with Daniel

Are you the boss of God?
You are the boss of God?
Nobody is the boss of God
Not me not you
Are the angels the boss of God?
Are you more famous than angels?
God orders himself
To do what he wants
I am the boss of this poem
I wrote it

9. A Lost Poem

> *"poems of Jesus"*
> —E. Pagels

I like to kiss Mary Magdalen on the mouth
and drink wine from her lips
and enter a cave without words
I am the song and the dove
And she is the rain and the question
Oh my students do not ask
Why do I kiss Mary on her lips
But rather
Why do I call myself a door?
An idiot knows the calendar
A wise man drinks wine from her lips
An idiot, I prepared the table for her
Now I prefer the Magdalen above my chief joy

10. Psalm

Lord, I am not too happy.
I am not looking too high.
I am not wasting my time
on the marvelous, too marvelous for me.
My mind is calm and quiet
like a quiet child on the breast;
my mind is like that quiet child.

Israel, you must hope
now and always.

11. For Borges: Spinoza

The luminous hands of an excommunicated Jew
Place a fly in the spider's web
And a spider next to another spider. They fight,
He laughs. This is not the ghetto's boundary.
A man comes to visit, then denies it.
His coat with the assassin's hole
Droops calmly from a chair. There is no evil,
And there is no good. He is dreaming
Of a bright light obvious labyrinth.
They have torn apart the de Witt brothers,
They are howling for his head. But now he rests
Coughing a little from the dust of the lens.
Heidelberg and the professorship he will turn down:
Better the private life, free like an insect
Fighting the relative fight. To endure
Like a stone growing conscious in its flight.
Like a worm in the blood. But now feeling everything
And knowing that we live forever, like a hyacinth.

12. An Evening Without Criticism

Comedy and Irony gave a poetry reading together
To stagger the public they recited by memory as *sound sculptors*
In a competitive fury full of confidence and metre
A long poem entitled I Am a Metaphor
Most of their words illegible in the speedy reading
And Pathos sat enraged brooding like a balcony
Was it a tautology to win by cheap populism
The socialites were screaming that the renga was sweet
And Pathos too approached and gave his false approval
It was the birthday of Comedy past middle age
Pathos dug through his pockets for a gift
And found some silver that seemed stolen a bent spoon-fork
He had wanted to introduce new cutlery into the West
To fabricate the old chair where one could not sit
And make his fortune writing fortune-cookies in countries that had none
Pathos couldn't even say how he felt—murderously leaving
    Comedy in the street

13. Problems of the Moon

Tonight the moon dreams much more lazily
Piled on her pillows like a big beauty
With her light, polite fingers she caressed
Before sleeping the contours of her breast

She devotes herself to dying and fainting for hours
On the satiny back of soft avalanches
And then into white visions she launches
Her eyes, which step up into the blue sky like flowers

Sometimes on this globe in her unoccupied laziness
She permits a furtive tear to drop
And then a real poet, who hates sleep

Puts this tear in his hand: it's so pale
With veined phyllotaxis like opal
He puts it inside: far from sunny eyes

(Baudelaire)

14. The Uncertainty

> *"There are no awards for showing
> your uncertainty in foreign policy"*
> —K<small>ISSINGER</small>

The, or in other words, an—
As Francesco's father said in bed
And sick. "Le   un."

    There are words in my dreams
    The truncated rhomboid
    Of Melancholy.

I was asked to roll it to each facet.
On each side words were carved
Like a magic square branded in silver:

    A bird flew into the painting room
    above the painter's head
    And he suddenly lifted his eyes and smote the window

    And said: Man and bird
    Or zealous bat stretched across my shoulders.
    Bird on a painter's shoulders. Never painted bird.

15. *A Private Embrace*

Dear Jimmy Schuyler
How beautiful your poems are.
When I asked Fairfield about them
He spoke of their disjointedness
I asked him whether he associated
That with schizophrenia
He said he did
I thought it a bit naive
Not that Fairfield could ever
Be characterized as *that*
And lapsed into a complaisant
Dissertation on quantum mechanics

I am amazed that I have given away
Two or three of your books
And will have to buy them again

I am amazed by your courage
As Kenneth would say
To say the things you do
As when you said to a friend
"Can't you be content with your wife and me?"
Would I have published that? What does it mean,
Too personal? Kenneth says,
If it's beautiful, publish it. Or:
If it's beautiful, I publish it.

Thank you for publishing it.

16. A Note and Poem by Joe Ceravolo in a Dream

*He was a poet of grammar
and a love poet and what
is more he showed the re-
lationship between grammar
and love. When he perturbed
syntax he seemed to in-
vert? reinvent? universe?
the possibilities of love
by making so many multiple
relations possible and/or
present or present tense.
He is a possibilist poet
entrances with its naive
or Utopian anti-grammar.*

...

History and happiness
Are similar:
They happened—
Or are **prone** to happen
Or will happen, burstingly.
Or: they have not happened.
O history o happiness.

Of belief
I love tall, twisted
Juniper
Who twisted them
Like a particle beaten
in a linear accelerator
The wind twisted them.

(What are)
Rocks' birthstones (Daddy)
Birds are the flowers
Of the sky
Bird birds
Like particles hurtling
Through a linear accelerator
O history o happiness.

17. A Desert Rose

—with Daniel

One day
I slept for
  a very long
  time
When I woke
  up
I checked
my flowers
But the
  flowers
  were all,
  all brown
I wanted to
  know what
this
flower is
So I brang
  it
to the museum
of natural
  history
They know
  a lot
  about
  rocks
They said
  it is
  a desert
  rose
  Flowers
  are the
  minerals
  on the earth
Flowers are the stars
on the earth
Rocks are the flowers
of the earth

MULTIPLE SUNS

"As our Sun gets older, it actually gets hotter and might eventually be green, even blue, but it will be yellow for a billion years or so at least . . ." —**The New York Times**
November 19, 1991

The red sun is so young and small and cool it shouts like a star
The green sun is happier than ever, in certitude and size
The blue sun is strained and explodes along the edges like vocal cords
But the yellow sun is old and hot and knows it will be yellow for a billion years

The red sun loves to perform in front of all others
The green sun shrinks humiliated in this warm body never released
The blue sun peaks in the spectrum with a hot face, your face
But the yellow sun questions all questions and explains nothing on stage

The red sun remembers "You will rest when you are dead and only then"
The green sun flashes on that elegant industrial object the blank page
The blue sun says nothing but I am exploding now
Still the yellow sun hurts your eyes through the burnt umber window for a year

Inside the red sun is a fireweed with one stem erect
Inside the green sun is the dark-brown engraver beetle with his obvious burrow
Inside the blue sun is the mature crow, consuming a newborn lamb
Inside the yellow sun is day and light and location and movement of music with no moons

The red sun is so callow unsown *en negligée*
The green sun grows insolent as a young poet praying *Noli me tangere*
The blue sun attacks all others in a language of brilliant *passado*
But the yellow sun wears its yellow helmet and circumscribes a homely fence

And I have seen the red sun open like a seed—popular spring—and close
And the green sun kneels nervously in a wounded space
To the blue sun loving his army and his standing army and his purple searchlights
But the yellow sun slipped away and was quiet for a billion years or so

Oh red sun cool yourself down and be my primary-colored one on paper for a child
Oh green sun grill me like timbral dissonance and a whole choir of women
Oh blue sun it is upon you I would write for contrast like the blue page
But yellow sun you are my silent sun for a billion years on one brown stem

Why shouldn't the red sun be red, when the brick wall stands in sepia and doubt?
What does the green sun point to if not the blue sun?
When will the blue sun say it in its heaven of unanswerable questions?
Must the yellow sun limp away and be a yellow wall and be sold at the roadside
 for a billion years?

An imperfect feather drew the red sun and the frame wanders
Pastel dust started the green sun and it is fixed by its own aging
    light
Water filled the blue sun in its film of grey
But oil made the yellow sun and all flesh and it will be flesh and
    light together
        for a billion years or so, at least

THE SEASONS

Summer

I saw the ruins of poetry,
Of a poetry
Of a parody and it was
Terraces and gardens
A mural bright as candy
With unconcealed light
The ceiling sprayed upon us
With a bit of the Atlantic
Fish leaping about a henotheism
That permits no friend
And leaves us happier
In the sand than in our room
You are not a little bird in the street
Protected by a stationary car
And protesting too little
Synthesize the aqueduct and
The tepidarium and the lion's pit
The sun stapled shut
The sun not a wandering error
Sunspots are hair
Sun from above or in the light's maw
The sun as a windshield and we drove to time's beach
The sun another snowman
A monkey for a child
Unkidnapped calm
Good day! good time! pulverized shore
At night, when everyone is writing
At night, when everyone is reading
Or learning to read in the dark
Time, with its patent pending
Half-eaten fruit of those
Who fear no lions
No weapons
No suspects, no motives
Walking down the beach on
Our heads: man and dog

Forced alike to swim in hurricanes
By the father, actually to dog paddle
Without a subject like a fireweed
Or a thistle
But the law we did not abide and carried by air
A single drop and I mean drop
Of a honeysuckle would satisfy me then
A cricket arises at the bottom of the lawn
Alone and vague it hesitates to mount the curb
A natural fire discovered in the grillework of these woods
The long column of summer days
Scornfully you lower all the eyelids
And we breathe together a long time

Autumn

A project and a lack of derealization
And a warehouse like a button
A facade in dark gray velvet
With strips of false marble lettering
Bending with the remover to remove
Absorbed into the sky like a gourd
My temporary window like a garden
And the stairwell split open
Into the interior view of a sieve
Of stairwells elaborate in cross section
And the axonometric of Charles Lindbergh
A mannikin feted in his aviator clothes
At the Salon of Autumn
With your hands full of women's
Accessories
And the President with his lips
In the frigidaires
And the tires rolling up at the annual
Automobile salon
Something enormous: the real estate
You did not buy
Sunspots bleeding beneath an oak
No floor
No young fate
The history of time-lapse photography
Is falling now
You cannot even take dictation like daughters
You have destroyed a little of everything
How dare you interrupt my house
Of empty pictures
Make music too loud to listen to
Want the bed too low
Don't want this to exist
Want me to become unconscious
Of too many colors

A house to sink
Violins without bridges
Pencils too heavy to be carried
Dictionaries stuck in the ground
And the violin lies on the long black piano and replies

Winter

Hard winter
Unlivable house
Unlivable snow
It is true January
However
My son is smiling in his sleep
After death there are extremes
Of temperature
An automobile is attached to the planet
And it sails the ice like a caravel
It is a word without songs
And one stops on the highway
To observe the snow's perspective
As the executions are executed
With a technical precision
Like Ricci's spiccati
And the dead slide sidewise
While the moon moves outward
Failing to grip the roadway
Like a bed sliding under the frame
Of a cloudless sky
February has clumped and intimated
That I find you in these halls
Of powerlessness
The fields are messier each day
Freezing water throttles the sky
We are idle, like a pair
Of wild cars on the highway
O northern widowed word
Ice like a sidewalk on the river
A difficult year
And the head emits a hot kind of hope
The truth a novel highway going round
The suburbs and ultimately I
Become part of myself not you and a gulf and sea
Held at precise angles to forbid us

Crypto-opponents to join
In natural darkness
Whose tied feet the imaginary rat gnawed through
In comatose sleep I saw you last
No cemetery holds you nor a single
Fire that I could burn
I pretend to approach your metal mouth,
You put it close to me
Brush your lips with ice
In a key he rarely chose the F sharp minor
You used to say Oh you could say anything

Spring

A boy who stayed awake
And what he saw
Very near as opposed to
To the west of everything
He kisses the bug
The charred blossoms of the dogwood
Family sculpture or
Family carving
My father would point to the
Anomalous forsythia
Because of this truthless
Encyclopedism
It is just as good to meet
A dog or a cat
What they left out: Anger
Sex and history
My grandfather died singing
Called the best death
As my father stayed at the music stand
Or the dancer wants to do
That new thing: dancing until the end
A construction site in sunlight
I had written: Superbia's loutish
Psychological best-of-horse show
Does your promise shine like a highway
Like an effaced green work on a wall
Singing and partly singing
I walked with my son a little way
I say good-bye but not enough
He whirls around I disappear
You need the shadow of a child
Like an avalanche
He was glad he had stayed awake
And he stayed awake to this day
You the chrysalis and I the traditional ancestor exploded like
    aluminum

Drawing After Summer

I saw the ruins of poetry, of a poetry
Of a parody and it was a late copy bright as candy.
I approach your metal mouth, you put it close to me.

By the long column of a summer's day
Like a pair of wild cars on the highway
I saw the ruins of poetry, of a poetry.

The doll within the doll might tell the story
Inside the store: the real estate you could not buy.
I approach your metal mouth, you put it close to me.

Violin lies on piano and makes reply.
Hunted words. Gathered sentences. Pencils too heavy to carry.
I saw the ruins of poetry, of a poetry.

The history of time-lapse photography
Is a student exercise. Throttle the sky.
I approach your metal mouth, you put it close to me.

The moon moves outward failing to grip the roadway.
I see you stuck in the ground like a dictionary.
I saw the ruins of poetry, of a poetry.
I approach your metal mouth, you put it close to me.